ALLSORTS
IN THE POND

by Miriam Moss

Macdonald

Factual Adviser: Michael Boorer,
London Zoo

Editors: Barbara Tombs, Carolyn Jones
Teacher Panel: Coryn Bendelow,
Sue Dobbinson, Frances Scott
Designer: Sally Boothroyd
Production: Rosemary Bishop

Illustrations
Nichola Armstrong 8–9, 20–21, 22–23, 24–25
Linda Birch 11BR, 12–13B, 19TR, 23TR, 27BR
Mandy Doyle 10–11, 12–13
Anna Hancock 6–7, 26–27, 28–29
Doreen McGuinness/The Garden Studio 14–15, 16–17, 18–19

A MACDONALD BOOK

© Macdonald & Co (Publishers) Ltd 1988

First published in Great Britain in 1988 by
Macdonald & Co (Publishers) Ltd
London & Sydney
A member of Maxwell Pergamon
Publishing Corporation plc

All rights reserved

Printed and bound in Spain by
Cronion S.A.

Macdonald & Co (Publishers) Ltd
Greater London House
Hampstead Road
London NW1 7QX

British Library Cataloguing in Publication Data
Moss, Miriam
  In the pond.—(Allsorts; 4).
  1. Pond flora—Juvenile literature
  2. Pond fauna—Juvenile literature
  I. Title   II. Series
574.92′9   QH98
ISBN 0-356-13454-7
ISBN 0-356-13787-2   Pbk

How to use this book

First look at the contents page opposite, to see if the subject you want is there. For instance, if you want to find out about frogs and toads, you will find the information on pages 20 and 21. At the end of the book you will find a word list. This explains some of the more difficult words found in this book. There is also an index. Use it if you want to find out about one particular thing. For instance, if you want to find out about swans, the index tells you there is something about them on page 9.

'Daddy Fell into the Pond' from *Collected Poems* by Alfred Noyes, is reprinted by permission of John Murray (Publishers) Ltd.

'Ode to a Goldfish' by Gyles Brandreth from *A Second Poetry Book* (Oxford University Press) is reprinted by permission of the author.

CONTENTS

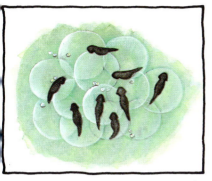

VISITING YOUR POND	6–7
POND BIRDS	8–9
POND PLANTS	10–11
FISH	12–13
SWIMMERS AND SKIMMERS	14–15
MAGIC CHANGES	16–17
CRAWLERS AND CLINGERS	18–19
FROGS, TOADS AND NEWTS	20–21
WATER MAMMALS	22–23
POND VISITORS	24–25
POLLUTED PONDS	26–27
THINGS TO DO	28–29
WORD LIST AND INDEX	30–31

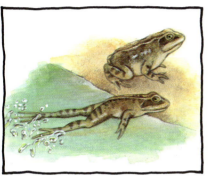

VISITING YOUR POND

A pond is a pool of still, shallow water. You find ponds wherever water is trapped and cannot run away. They are the homes of many animals and plants. Ponds can be all sorts of sizes. Even puddles and ditches sometimes have pond life in them. Most ponds are made by humans. Some village ponds were dug a long time ago for cattle to drink from. Others were made when rain filled chalk and gravel pits.

A pond full of life needs plenty of sunlight so that green plants can grow. Plants make oxygen so that animals can breathe. The best time to look for pond life is in the spring and summer.

Large pond animals eat smaller ones. The small animals eat the plants.

This picture shows some pond creatures. Can you guess what eats what?

Try to keep your plants and animals cool in the shade. It is unkind to put a lot of animals together in a small container.

Pond dipping can be great fun. You need to wear wellingtons or old plimsolls and to take this pond kit.

When you catch animals in your net, put them into tubs half-filled with pond water. It is easier to look at very small animals and plants with a hand lens.

You can find small animals and eggs under leaves. Worms, leeches and insects hide under stones. The water spider lives in an air bubble on plant stems.

Daddy Fell into the Pond

Everyone grumbled. The sky was grey.
We had nothing to do and nothing to say.
We were nearing the end of a dismal day.
And there seemed to be nothing beyond,
   Then
      Daddy fell into the pond!

And everyone's face grew merry and bright,
And Timothy danced for sheer delight.
"Give me the camera, quick, oh quick!
He's crawling out of the duckweed!" Click!

Then the gardener suddenly slapped his knee,
And doubled up, shaking silently,
And the ducks all quacked as if they were daft,
And it sounded as if the old drake laughed.
Oh, there wasn't a thing that didn't respond
   When
      Daddy fell into the pond!

Alfred Noyes

POND BIRDS

Many birds come to the pond to feed and to make their nests. Migrating birds visit the pond in winter and spring. Some arrive in groups called flocks. Geese arrive flying in a V shape. They call to each other and make a loud honking noise. Mallards fly in a straight line.

Pond birds come in lots of different shapes and sizes. A heron is nearly a metre tall. A reed warbler almosts fits into your hand. Some pond birds have webbed feet. This means they have skin between their toes which helps them to paddle through the water. When you are birdwatching remember to be very quiet or you will frighten the birds away.

Little grebes can swim soon after they are born. Sometimes they climb on to their parents' backs to keep safe from danger.

Reed warblers hide in the reeds at the water's edge. In winter they fly to Africa where it is warmer. Can you find out how far they travel?

The tufted duck dives under water to catch insects. Only the male has the tuft of feathers on its head. Can you draw a tufted duck?

The heron is a tall, silent bird. It spears fish and frogs with its long, sharp beak. The heron's long legs trail out behind as it flies.

When a swan flies overhead you can hear its wings beating loudly.

Swans can be very fierce. They puff up their feathers and hiss to frighten away enemies.

The moorhen's long toes spread out wide to help it walk on floating lily leaves and soft mud. Moorhens sink under water when they are scared. Only their beaks show. Can you see any moorhens hiding?

These outlines show the birds on this page. Can you guess which are which? Look at their size and shape and the way they fly.

Birds with short wings flap their wings fast. Birds that fly with their necks stretched out and their feet trailing, fly slowly.

POND PLANTS

Animals cannot live in a pond without plants. Plants make oxygen for animals to breathe. Some plants provide food and shelter for animals and birds. Ponds need plants. It is very important not to pick too many from one place. Just take a small part of the plant if you want to look up its name.

Plants can be big or small. One kind of grass can grow as tall as a single decker bus! Green algae are so tiny that they look like green slime on the water. Plants that grow in deep water don't need strong stems. The water holds them up. Plants in shallow water have thick stems.

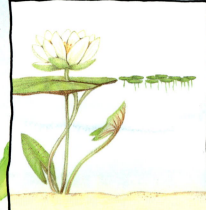

Water lilies grow in deep water, rooted in mud. Thousands of tiny floating duckweed plants can cover the whole pond. Their roots hang free.

common reed

great reedmace

These plants grow in the mud in the shallow water around the edge of the pond. The dark brown top of the great reedmace is made of thousands of tiny seeds. How do you think these tiny seeds travel to find somewhere to root?

forget-me-not   marsh marigold

These plants grow in the soft, damp soil on the bank of the pond. Many of the plants here have large leaves and strong roots. Plants like rushes and sedge can grow taller than an adult (up to 200cm). Others, like the forget-me-not, have colourful flowers. Why do you think this is?

soft rush   great pond sedge

When plants grow they use sunlight to make oxygen. Try an experiment. Put some Canadian pondweed in a glass bowl of water in the sun. What happens? What else can you see in the bowl after a little while?

water plantain
water crowfoot

A pond may be deep. If you want to wade in, test the depth with a pole first. *Never* go in if you can't swim – and don't go to a pond alone.

Some plants grow under water in the middle of the pond. Spiked water milfoil has long stems under the water and flower spikes above the surface. Canadian pondweed grows so quickly that it can choke other plants.

Canadian pondweed
spiked water milfoil

FISH

Fishes living in ponds can be very different sizes. The eel looks like a long water-snake. The pike can be as long as an ironing board. The minnow is only as long as your little finger. Most fish spawn in shallow water. Spawning means laying eggs.

If you catch a fish in your net, try not to touch it. Put it straight into a large bowl of pond water. What colour is it? Does it swim near the surface or near the bottom? Does it have whiskers, called barbels, for feeding and tasting? Don't forget to return the fish to the pond.

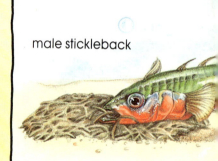

male stickleback

In spring the male stickleback builds a nest from reed stems. He does a zig-zag dance to show the female his nest. She lays her eggs in it.

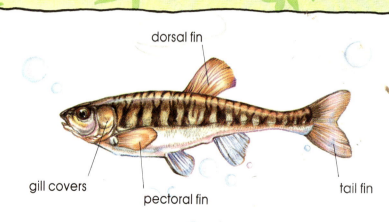

dorsal fin
gill covers
pectoral fin
tail fin

This picture of a minnow shows what the different parts of a fish are called.

Have you noticed that fish open and close their mouths and gill covers?

This is how they breathe. They take water in through their mouths and pass it over their gills. The gills take oxygen from the water. Do you have to open your mouth to breathe?

female stickleback

The eggs hatch into tiny fry. The male guards the fry. He chases away enemies and if the fry stray off, he brings them back to the nest in his mouth.

Carp have feelers at the sides of their mouths which help them to find food. They suck up mud and filter out the food in it. Tench often lie buried in the mud. They eat insects and snails.

The pike is very fierce. It hunts ducklings, fishes, frogs, and even other pike. Its colour and pattern helps it to hide in the reeds. It watches for food. Then it attacks with its sharp teeth.

Ode to a Goldfish

O
Wet
Pet

Gyles Brandreth

Fish can feel you moving along the bank. They can see your shadow if it falls on the water. If you want to see fish you have to walk up to the pond very slowly and quietly.

SWIMMERS AND SKIMMERS

Different animals live in different parts of the pond. Dip your net half in the water and half out of it to catch the animals which live at the surface. Skimming insects live on top of the water. A thin skin or layer on the surface of the water, called surface tension, holds the insects up. Watch the surface carefully. Can you see which skimming animal whizzes about like a dodgem car? Which one jumps about like a flea?

All the surface animals dart away if the surface of the water is disturbed. Why do you think this is?

Some swimmers breathe air at the surface. Others collect a bubble of oxygen and carry it under water on their bodies. When the oxygen is used up, they return to the surface for more.

These tiny animals drift near the surface of the water. They are sometimes called water fleas. You need to use an eyedropper to move them and a hand lens to study them.

Water beetles, water boatmen and water scorpions are fierce hunters. If you catch one of these animals, keep it by itself and feed it on meat.

The great diving beetle often eats animals larger than itself, like tadpoles and fishes. The water boatman is a fierce hunter and a strong swimmer. It swims on its back under water.

whirligig beetle

springtail

pond skater

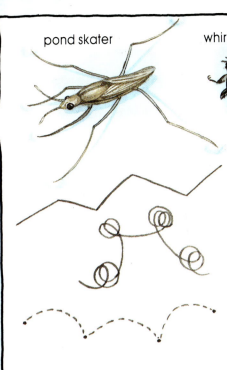

Pond skaters eat other insects. They can feel with their feet when an insect falls into the water. Tiny spring tails jump using their hinged tails. Whirligig beetles whirl and spin while looking for food.

Which animals make these patterns when they skim?

The water scorpion's long tail is a breathing tube. It sucks in air at the surface. The water measurer has hairs on its body to stop it getting wet. It catches tiny animals with its sharp beak.

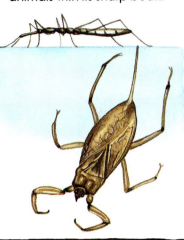

A thin skin called surface tension holds skimmers up. Try this experiment to see how well it works. Put a piece of blotting paper with a needle resting on it gently on the surface of a bowl of water. What happens to the blotting paper and the needle?

MAGIC CHANGES

Some pond insects go through amazing changes before they become adults. When they hatch from eggs they are called larvae or nymphs. Many nymphs spend years under water crawling around in the mud, eating plants or catching insects. Then they stop eating and become very still. Their bodies slowly change. When they are ready, they climb out of the water and split their old skins. Some change into beautiful dragonflies that hover in the air above the pond. Some insects only live for a few hours or days as adults. What other animals change from crawlers into flying insects?

You can tell different insects apart if you look at them closely. What colour are they? How many wings do they have?

great silver beetle   caddis fly   gnat

Insects lay their eggs in spring. Some of the eggs look very strange! You can find the great silver beetle's eggs in a silky covering called a cocoon.

Caddis fly eggs are laid in jelly stuck to plants. The gnat lays tiny rafts of eggs which float on the water. The rafts are only as wide as your little finger nail.

The china mark moth larva lies underneath water lily leaves, eating them. Look in the mud for the rat-tailed maggot. Mosquito larvae hang under the water breathing through a tube.

When the caddis fly larva hatches from an egg it makes itself a case of stones, shells or leaves. It feeds at the bottom of the pond.

After about a year the larva stops eating and goes into its case. It slowly changes into an adult. Then it moves to the surface, splits out of its old skin and flies away.

The young dragonfly is called a nymph. It will attack almost anything with its mask. This is a hooked bottom jaw.

The nymph lives under water for up to four years. When the nymph is ready it climbs up a stalk out of the water. Its skin bursts open and an adult dragonfly pulls itself out. It waits until its wings open, then it flies off.

mosquito larva

china mark moth larva

rat-tailed maggot

CRAWLERS AND CLINGERS

You will find crawlers and clingers at the bottom of the pond. Dip for these animals last. This is because dipping at the bottom stirs up the mud and makes it difficult to see the other animals in the pond. The mud in the bottom of the pond is very important. Plants root themselves in it and animals shelter in it during the cold winter months.

When twigs and leaves drop into a pond, they fall to the bottom and start to rot. The animals on this page feed on these rotting plants. Only animals that don't need much oxygen live down at the bottom of the pond. Look under stones for worms, insects and leeches. Try to put the stones back where you found them.

The ramshorn snail feeds by licking algae off stones and plants with its rough, rasping tongue. It also eats partly rotted plants from the bottom of the pond.

Put some pond water in a glass jar. Leave it for a few weeks until green algae grows on the sides of the jar. Then put in a pond snail. You can watch it feeding on the algae. It moves across the glass using its strong, muscular foot.

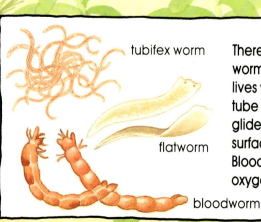

There are lots of different worms. The tubifex worm lives with its head down a tube of mud. The flatworm glides easily over the surface of rocks. Bloodworms can store oxygen in their bodies.

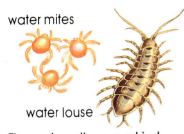

Tiny water mites are a kind of spider. The water louse crawls along the bottom over dead leaves and stones. It holds its food with its front legs.

You can use a sieve to hold your catch while you wash the mud off. Put the animals back in the pond when you have looked at them. The best way is to float them in a spoon on the surface.

The horse leech uses its suckers to move along while it stretches and loops its body. It swims gracefully. When it is disturbed it shrinks into a blob.

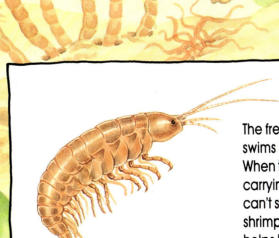

The freshwater shrimp swims by flicking its tail. When the female shrimp is carrying a lot of eggs, she can't swim easily. The male shrimp holds on to her and helps her swim along.

FROGS, TOADS AND NEWTS

Frogs, toads and newts will disappear with a plop at the slightest sign of any danger. You have to sit very quietly if you want to see them. Frogs, toads and newts are called amphibians. They all hatch in water but spend most of their adult life on land.

Amphibians are cold-blooded. They need the sun to warm them and make them active. In winter when it is cold and there is less food, they hibernate. This means they sleep through the cold months, hiding in the mud or in holes.

This snake cannot swallow the toad because the toad has puffed itself up. The toad also has poison on its skin. How do other animals frighten away enemies?

Frogs lay thousands of eggs in jelly which floats on the water. The sun warms them. You can see the little tadpoles in the eggs. Toads lay long ribbons of eggs. Newts lay single eggs on leaves under water.

After about ten days the tadpole wriggles out of the egg. It breathes through gills and stays underwater. Over several weeks it grows legs and loses its tail. It grows lungs to breathe air. Now it is a tiny frog.

In spring the male newt attracts females with his bright colours and crest. You might be lucky enough to see a male newt among the plants dancing to a female. He arches his back and flicks his tail.

spadefoot toad

fire-bellied toad

parsley frog

great crested newt

natterjack toad

These are some of the interesting amphibians which live in Britain and Europe. Some of them are brightly coloured. The great crested newt is colourful to attract females. The fire-bellied toad shows its red colour when it is alarmed.

WATER MAMMALS

Many other water animals live in and around ponds. Can you spot the clues which show where they live? See if you can find holes in the banks belonging to water rats, water shrews and water voles. Look among the reeds for a harvest mouse's nest made of leaves woven into a ball.

Feeding signs are another clue. Nibbled plant stems show where water voles feed. Bird feathers might show where an otter or a mink has been hunting. Can you find animal tracks on a shallow muddy bank? Try drawing the tracks and the pattern that they make. Then see if you can work out which animals they belong to.

The otter has waterproof fur and webbed toes for swimming. It shuts its ears and nostrils when it dives under water to catch frogs and fish. Otter cubs are born in a hole in the bank, called a holt.

The tiny water shrew has a grey velvety coat. Sometimes it walks along the bottom of the pond looking for food. It eats frogs, fish, insects and worms.

The best way to see pond mammals is to creep up to the water very quietly. Make sure that you face the wind. If you don't, the animals will smell you and hide.

Many harvest mice build their nests in the reeds around ponds. Harvest mice are very good climbers – they can even hang by their tails!

You can see animal tracks most clearly when the ground is covered in firm mud or snow. Can you guess which animals these tracks belong to?

The water vole often swims under the water. You might see a water vole sitting on floating water plants and cleaning its fur.

POND VISITORS

The pond is different at night, when it is dark and cold. The pond plants stop making food and the temperature of the water drops. At night most of the tiny water animals do not sleep, but they stop moving. They hide among the plants or rest at the bottom of the pond.

In the dark some of the larger land animals come to the pond to hunt, or drink. These animals often have very good hearing and a strong sense of smell to warn them of danger.

The tawny owl flies silently. This helps it to catch voles and mice. The owl sleeps all day and comes out to hunt at night.

The puss moth has a thick, furry body which feels like cats' fur. It flies at night, feeding in the trees around the pond.

At night the fox creeps up to the pond sniffing the air. She wants to catch a frog or steal an egg from a nest for her cubs. If there is no sign of any food, she will slide away into the shadow of the trees.

The bats flap their leathery wings over the pond. They sleep all day in special places called roosts. They cannot see very well but they have such good hearing that they can catch flying insects in the dark.

The grass snake slides silently from its hole. It has come out to hunt for frogs, toads, newts and fish. It swims fast and gracefully.

The hedgehog snuffles around the pond's edge looking for insects to eat. If it senses danger, it rolls up into a ball for protection.

A deer comes nervously up to the pond to drink. It is listening for danger. Its hooves make clear tracks, like pairs of slots, in the muddy bank.

POLLUTED PONDS

When poisons or unhealthy things get into a pond we call it pollution. Pollution will harm the animals and plants in the pond. Sometimes it kills all the plants straight away. Then the animals have nothing to eat. Sometimes pollution makes one plant grow so quickly that it chokes all the other plants. Most animals and plants will die if their pond is polluted.

Pollution can happen if a factory puts poisonous waste into ponds and streams. Fertilizers can cause pollution if they get into the pond. Sometimes people even use ponds as rubbish dumps. Do you think it is important to stop pollution? Why?

Factories often produce poisonous waste. Sometimes this spills into rivers. It kills the fish, plants and animals.

Factory chimneys burning coal and oil puff acid smoke up into the air. The acid comes down again when it rains. Acid rain falls on the countryside and into ponds, killing plants and animals.

Farmers spray their crops with fertilizers. The wind and rain spread them into ponds. They can kill pond plants and animals.

If you think a pond may be polluted, look for these animals. If you see stonefly nymphs, the pond is healthy. If the only animals you can find are mosquito larvae, rat-tailed maggots or bloodworms then the water is polluted. If there are no animals or plants, the water must be very badly polluted.

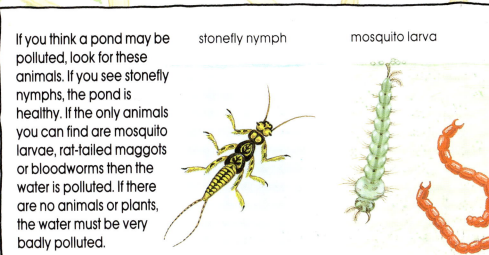

stonefly nymph

mosquito larva

rat-tailed maggot

bloodworms

Ponds need light. The pond plants and animals will die if thick overhanging trees block out the light and all their leaves fall into the water.

You can help stop ponds from becoming polluted. Always put your rubbish in a bin or take it home with you.

THINGS TO DO

KEEPING A POND DIARY

Visit a pond every few weeks for a whole year. Write down the plants, animals and birds you see there, and draw them. Keep a diary describing each of your visits. How does the pond change at different times of the year?

MAKING A POND VIEWER

Take a large empty tin and use a can opener to remove the top and the bottom. Tape over the cut edges. Use a rubber band to hold a piece of clear plastic over one end. Put this covered end into the water and look through the open end.

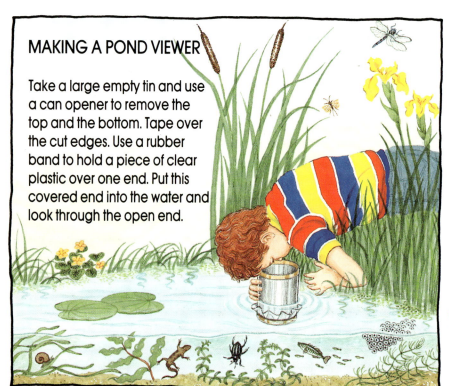

MAKING A MAP OF THE POND

Get some friends or an adult to help you measure across and around the pond with a tape measure. Draw the shape on a large sheet of paper. Draw on your map the main landmarks around the pond, like trees. What is the bottom of the pond made of – mud, clay, sand or gravel? Write down the names of all the different animals and plants you find, and put them on your map.

HATCHING GNATS AND MOSQUITOES

In summer look for gnats' and mosquitoes' egg rafts. You will find them on the surface of ponds, in forgotten buckets of water and in water which collects in hollow trees. Keep some of the eggs outside, in a jar of the water that you found them in. The eggs hatch into tiny larvae after a few days. After about three weeks the larvae start to change into adult gnats or mosquitoes which finally fly away. Try to draw the eggs, larva and adult insects.

MAKING A NET

You can make a pond dipping net by cutting one leg off an old pair of tights. Sew the open end on to a strong loop of wire. Fit the wire into the end of a bamboo cane. If you want to catch very tiny animals, you need to cut off the "foot" of your net and fix in a test tube. Make a small wire loop. Thread the end of the net through it. Push the test tube inside.

MAKING AN AQUARIUM

Any bowl can be used to make an aquarium for freshwater animals to live in, but a glass tank is best. Wash the tank, gravel and stones very carefully. Put a sloping layer of gravel over the bottom of the tank. Add some large hard stones.

Root plants like pond weed and water milfoil in the gravel using the larger stones. Protect the plants with a piece of newspaper while you pour on pond water. The water must stand for a day to let the mud settle. Leave the tank water to settle again for at least a week. Now put your animals in. Remember that certain animals will attack others if you put them together. Find out whether any of your animals need special food. Keep your aquarium near a window but not in full sunlight.

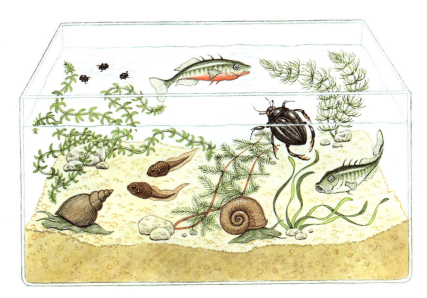

WORD LIST

acid rain: when acid smoke from factory chimneys falls in the rain.

algae: very simple green plants that look like green slime.

amphibian: a cold-blooded animal which breeds in water and can live on land, like frogs, toads and newts.

aquarium: a large glass tank used to keep fish, water animals and plants.

barbels: whiskers or feelers that hang from fishes' mouths to help them to feed and taste.

fertilizer: something that farmers spray on their crops to help them to grow.

flock: a group of birds.

fry: tiny, newly hatched baby fish

gills: part of a fish. Gills are usually on the sides of the head. They are used for breathing. Fish don't have lungs like land animals. Their gills take oxygen from the water.

hand lens: a small magnifying glass.

hibernate: to stay asleep during the winter.

larva: the feeding stage in the life of an insect hatched from an egg. The name for more than one larva is larvae.

mammals: warm-blooded animals. The mothers feed their babies with milk.

mask: the dragonfly nymph's hooked bottom jaw.

migrating birds: birds who fly south to a warmer place in winter. They go north again for the summer.

nymph: the name given to the young of insects like dragonflies.

oxygen: a gas in the air which living things need to live.

pollution: dirt or poison that makes a pond unhealthy.

pond: a pool of still water.

spawn: the eggs of fishes and other egg-laying water animals, like frogs and toads.

surface tension: a thin skin on the surface of the water.

tracks: the prints of an animal's feet in soft or wet ground.